Self-Reliance, Translated

Ralph Waldo Emerson's
Self-Reliance Translated
Into Modern English

Translator: Adam Khan

Published in the USA

YouMe Works Publishing

DEDICATION

To Klassy Evans, my wife and business partner,
who embodies the principles set forth so
eloquently by Emerson. She is a living example
of honesty and authenticity.

ACKNOWLEDGMENTS

I would like to thank Rudolf Flesch for the principles he discovered about readability.

INTRODUCTION

THE FOLLOWING IS Ralph Waldo Emerson's essay, *Self-Reliance*, translated into modern English. I've been studying this essay for years. I consider it one of the most significant pieces of writing ever published.

I once typed the whole essay word for word and printed it as a booklet for myself because I couldn't find a version of the book that stood alone — it was always in a collection of essays. I wanted only *Self-Reliance*.

While I was at it, I looked up all the words I didn't know and made footnotes of definitions for each word on the page (and there were a lot of them).

Then I recorded the essay and listened to it over and over whenever I drove my car. And I tried to apply its insights to my life.

Then, to understand it even better, I went over it line by line, trying to write what Emerson wrote in my own words. That rewrite project is what follows.

I don't think I'm a better writer than Emerson. I love his writing. Some of his sentences were so well said, I included them in this translation just because I couldn't bear to leave them out. My motivation for "translating" it came from an experience I had with *Cliff Notes*.

I had always considered *Cliff Notes* as a kind of cheating. If you didn't want to read the real book, you could read a condensed version that tells you everything you need to know to pass a test. Then one day I saw the movie *Henry V* (the one with Kenneth Branagh). I really liked it but I only understood about half of what they were saying. They were speaking English, but three things were hindering my understanding:

1. English was spoken differently back then. They commonly used words we are now unfamiliar with.

2. Shakespeare was a poet, so he often inverted sentences and used unusual phrases in order to make the writing poetic.

3. They were speaking with an English accent.

Emerson's essay is *difficult* for a modern English speaker for the first two reasons. Emerson used words that, although I can find them in a dictionary, I never hear anyone say them. And he was a poet, so some of his phrases were meant to be savored rather than read only for their direct meaning.

Just by chance, I was browsing in a used bookstore one day when I came across a *Cliff Notes* on *Henry V* and I was curious about what it might say, so I read it and found it a *revelation.* It explained terms and phrases I didn't know.

For example, it explained the phrase, "throwing down a gage." It's an archaic term that means throwing your gloves at someone's feet, which in those days meant you were challenging the person to a duel. After I learned it, I understood better what was going on when I watched the movie again.

That's what I hope happens to you when you read my translation. I hope you go back and enjoy Emerson's original and eloquent essay, and understand it better, and really appreciate his creative, powerful prose.

When I tell people about translating Emerson, the first thing people always ask me is, "Why would his work need to be 'translated?' After all, he lived a fairly short time ago and he spoke English."

I've found when I share a quote or two from Emerson, it becomes clear why such a translation might be helpful. For example, this is from the original *Self-Reliance*:

> "As soon as he has once acted or spoken with éclat he is a committed person, watched by the sympathy or the hatred of hundreds, whose affections must now enter into his account. There is no Lethe for this. Ah, that he could pass again into his neutral, godlike independence! Who can thus lose all pledge and, having observed, observe again from the same unaffected, unbiased, unbribable, unaffrighted innocence, must always be formidable, must always engage the poet's and the man's regards."

I enjoy Emerson's prose. But it took some time and I had to look up a few words before I really understood what he was saying in that paragraph. A translation really helps.

Here, then, is my translation of Ralph Waldo Emerson's essay, *Self-Reliance.*

SELF-RELIANCE,
TRANSLATED

THE OTHER DAY, I read some original statements written by a famous painter. Whenever I read something truly original, I get a feeling and that feeling is far more valuable than the statements themselves. The feeling fills me with a recognition of a profound truth: That genius is simply to "believe your own thought." "To believe that what is true for you in your private heart is true for all [people]."

Speak what is true for you, and it will almost always resonate in others.

The voice in your own mind is so familiar to you that you give it no respect. Instead, you give too much weight to the thoughts of others — your neighbors, your teachers, or some great thinker from the past. But what made those great thinkers "great" is that they did *not* disregard their own thoughts. They *expressed* what they *truly* thought; they listened to their own voice.

You must learn to detect the light that shines from within and pay it more respect than the blinding illumination of the great minds of history. When you look at wonderful works of art, let it teach you this.

Let the flashes of genius that hit your mind urge you to stick with your own "spontaneous impression with good-humored inflexibility" — especially when everyone seems to think otherwise. Speak out what your own perception, your own impression tells you is true, and speak with boldness and trust.

As Emerson wrote, "envy is ignorance; imitation is suicide." You have something unique, original, and great to express. Try to imitate someone else and you kill off that originality *which is you*. Envy is a lack of appreciation of your own special gifts.

Nobody knows what your gifts really are, and *you* won't know until you try to express them. Follow your own interest. It will lead you where you need to go.

You are an expression of this vast and wondrous universe. *You* are one of the things the universe is doing right now. This immense, mysterious existence is expressing itself everywhere at every moment. For the miracle to be expressed through you, it will take courage and a firm dedication to truth and honesty. The greatness of the universe cannot be expressed by cowards.

Be brave and true to yourself. Put your heart into your work. Do these things with sincerity and you come nearer to being what you truly are: A singular expression of all existence — a genius, a creator, a redeemer, a healer, a teacher, a force for good in the world.

Trust yourself — not your petty self, but that Self you touch in blissful solitude on quiet walks in the mountains, that Self you are when you rise to a challenge, that Self you feel when you are at your highest best.

Completely accept your current situation — the place and time you live in. Accept it and make something magnificent with it. There is no better time. There is nothing to wish for. Genius and wisdom arise when you see that the source of existence is in your heart and works through your hands.

You are not a victim of life. You have a destiny, a part to play in this awesome universal battle between good and evil. Step forth and follow your destiny, no matter what anyone else says.

Look at children. They trust their own impression. They haven't learned to calculate how many people oppose their purposes and so they don't alter their purposes accordingly. If they conceive a purpose, they start to accomplish it without any self-censoring calculations.

Infants do not conform. The adults conform to the infant. An infant is charming, attractive, interesting, and the adults gather around and try to please him or her. But listen: There is something just as charming, just as interesting, and just as pleasing about every stage of life, from childhood to old age. Infancy has no monopoly on charm.

Take exactly what you are, find the magnificence of it, and express it. Do not weep for younger years or think things will be great only when you get older. Be exactly what you are right now and already your charm begins to manifest itself.

It is a healthy attitude to consider conciliatory behavior beneath you. In other words, don't try to gain goodwill by displaying pleasing behavior. Don't try to beg for peoples' approval. That is the attitude of someone who doesn't feel he has a right to be what he is, to feel the way he feels, to think what he thinks. But you *do* have the right.

Be yourself.

Don't try to figure out what behavior or opinion will make you popular with others. It is disrespectful to the grandeur of who you really are. It is selling your soul for the low outcome of manipulating the superficial affections of others — as if you needed their approval. Be what you are. Be indifferent to the judgments of others, not with a thoughtless or angry defiance, but with the firm knowledge that you are a vital expression of something unspeakably intelligent and good.

Forget about what you have been before. Forget what you've said before. Be what you are now, even if it "isn't you" — that is, even if it seems to contradict what you or others have pigeonholed you to be. Be free. Be the creative force on the crest of the mighty wave of this very instant.

Be exactly what you are right now and what will happen? Your truth, your honesty, will scare some people, and they will actively try to make you stop being true to yourself.

The world is in a conspiracy to make you conform. Others will think they know what you should be and how you should act and what you should think. And they will apply pressure to you to make you conform to it.

But if you conform, you lose your soul. You lose your originality. You lose your connection to the Mystery. You lose your creativity and your aliveness.

The people who know you will sometimes resist your creativity. They feel more comfortable with what is familiar.

If you want to be the full greatness you can be, you must care less about what others think and be your honest self. As Emerson put it, "Nothing is at last sacred but the integrity of your own mind." Rely on yourself and you become one of those who determine the future of the world.

Not you? Why *not* you? Many of the people who have changed the course of history also would not have believed that they could or would. But when you rely on yourself and be *exactly* what you are, a new force moves through you, and a new source of power backs your efforts.

Emerson said, "No law can be sacred to me but that of my nature. Good and bad are but names very readily transferable to that or this; the only right is what is after my constitution; the only wrong what is against it." Take the stand that *you* are the one who knows, and all opposing people and opinions are only temporary fads and "authority" propped up by the mere agreement of mob mentality.

"Go upright and vital," urges Emerson, "and speak the rude truth in all ways." When you hear someone earnestly spouting the latest politically correct opinion, why not be direct and without apology say, "I don't want to hear a popular opinion. What do *you* really think and why?" This response might be taken as somewhat rude, but honesty is far more beautiful than the pretense of acceptance, and it will do more good. Conditions do not improve when everyone goes along just to avoid seeming rude.

Emerson wrote, "For nonconformity, the world whips you with its displeasure…but the sour face of the multitude, like their sweet faces, have no deep cause…but are put on and off as the wind blows and the newspaper directs." Have the fortitude to treat this displeasure "as a trifle of no concernment." The displeasure is really beneath your notice.

The reason conformity is so damaging is that it "scatters your force." It takes the pure, strong, true expression you are and blurs it into feebleness and mediocrity.

But go about your business with a deep honesty, and your power shines through, your genius arises, your true goodness has a chance to show itself, and your creativity is charged with new force.

Do not join any crowd. Every club or group tries to make each member a "retained attorney," locked into one perspective, chained to a set of beliefs that blind you to the truth. You can no longer just see. You are driven to justify a certain point of view, to uphold a fixed perspective, cutting away your freedom and cutting you off from a free expression of the immense intelligence you really are.

As a painful example of the sensation of being locked away from your own soul, consider the feeling you get when talking to people you don't feel comfortable with, wearing a forced smile, a painful smile, while you converse on topics that don't interest you. It makes your face hurt. The discomfort is a clear signal. In your dishonesty you have stuffed a towel into the tube through which your life and creative force flow, leaving you without power or com-fort or peace or happiness.

Follow your deep whim. Do what you truly want to do — not your superficial, thoughtless impulses, but when you are here, now, being as nakedly honest with yourself as you can, speak and act from that unmasked honesty and your perceptions and creations will strike a chord in the hearts of others, for the center of their Self converges with the center of yours.

People do and say things much of the time in the spirit of someone trying to make amends or atone for a sin. They take actions as if to justify or excuse themselves. Their whole demeanor reeks of apology.

But I need no excuse. I'm not here to please the world. I'm here to *live*. My life exists as an end in itself, without needing justification. My life is for itself and not for a show.

If my motivations are base, so be it. Better that they are base and honest than lofty and phony.

My life should be unique and original. It should not be like any other and no apology is needed for that. Act from the center and your life is a saving grace, a triumph, a work of art, a cavalry charging over the hill to win the day.

You have the right to be what you are. Never allow well-meaning people to make you pay for that privilege. You are what you are and you need no stamp of approval or sponsor to grant you the authority to be so.

All that needs to concern you is your own task, not what people think about it or you. This is difficult and may be the only defining difference between those who are great and those who are mediocre.

When you are alone, it's easy to be yourself. When among your fellows, you are bent, pulled, and pushed by their desire for you to be this or that, and by your own desire to be accepted and appreciated. Do your best to keep your solitary independence when among others.

Trust yourself. Don't concern yourself with what you have said or done in the past. Others have seen it and expect you, even *insist* that you act that way in the future.

Set yourself free. Learn and grow and extend your understanding. Create yourself newly, freshly, honestly. When your soul is moved, yield to it, even if it contradicts what you knew or thought in the past.

Do not try to be consistent. Trying to be consistent blocks the new creation that constantly wants to flow out of you.

Yes, you will be misunderstood. All great souls have suffered this indignity. You'll be in excellent company. You will be a *cause*, a *creator*, an *architect* of a new world, as all great souls have been who had the guts to see the world with honest eyes, and the courage to speak truthfully.

Act and speak from that honest place and when you look closely at what you've done, it may seem you spout contradictory statements while you try to express the sometimes profound paradox the truth encompasses. The course of a missile looks like a zigzag up close because it is constantly correcting its flight path. But when you look at it from a distance it flies straight and true to its mark. In the very same way, you will find that your honest expression will have a deeper, more intelligent trajectory than you could have realized from so close a perspective.

Our puny conscious mind cannot see the big picture. Our feeble efforts of willpower are completely outmatched by the grandeur of the will of the universe, and to second-guess it or to think you can edit it in-flight is the arrogance of the ignorant. *Give up your effort to censure yourself.* Be an honest, open expression and you will be surprised at the height of your knowing in the long run.

Be great enough to be true now, with self-trust, with self-reliance, with self-sufficiency, independent of your own pet theories or the scolding fingers of others.

Trust yourself and shine from the center and the works you produce will justify you in the end.

HEROES

The force of your independent character is surrounded by, as it were, an escort of angels

— you are surrounded by all the great souls of history who have defied the status quo and acted from the source.

We respect and admire the brave heroes of the past because they were true to themselves. And in the end we will respect and honor those who do it now. Courage is not superficial. It is eternal and transcendent and that's what makes it great. The courageous do not try to please or appease, they do not try to win our respect, and so ultimately win it.

Cultivate a profound indifference to circumstances, opinions, and authority. Do this and future generations will bring your original work to its full fruition. The world will follow you.

The reading of human history is the reading of the biographies of a few strong people who took resolute action, often against tremendous popular resistance — resistance to noncomformity, resistance to genuine, original thoughts and actions.

Know your worth and keep your feet on the ground. Do not sneak around, afraid, as if you had no right to be what you are. Know your true worth and allow the source to express itself through you.

You see great works — statues, buildings, machines, books, and you feel belittled by them, put in your place, puny, unworthy. But you're looking at it all wrong. Their greatness awaits *your* judgment. Emerson wrote, "The picture waits for my verdict; it is not to command me, but I am to settle its claims to praise."

The state of humankind is like a king who has forgotten his place and wanders the world like a beggar. Don't make that mistake! Wake up, be what you are, and express your genius and originality.

Do not envy or feel inferior when you read of a great soul. So they were great. So what? Did they *use up* greatness? No! Your own actions have as much potential to affect the future if you would be exactly what you are — fully and truly.

When you express *your* unique gifts, the honor will be transferred to you just as readily.

Great souls have existed at all times since the beginning. There are no fewer great souls now than have ever been. In fact, the number is probably greater if the percentage stayed the same.

You will find a startling similarity between all self-reliant souls of history, no matter what time and place they lived. What they share is that the great souls leave behind no classification into which others may fit. Anyone who is truly in the same category will not seem similar, but will be wholly unique.

We should look at the reverence we give to presidents and statesmen and the supersuccessful and realize it is the level of respect we should give to ourselves. These great people were ordinary folks who decided to take matters into their own hands, to fulfill their destinies — sometimes at great personal cost. Each of us also has a latent greatness if we would only break free of conformity.

THE SOURCE

All original action has an undeniable magnetism. Why? Think about it: The source of those original actions is the center and source of all things. That center is what can be trusted. *That center* is the source of genius, of moral strength, of self-discipline, and the source of all life and all aliveness.

At the center of you is the center of all things. That source of being and wisdom is not separate from other things but emanates and expresses itself as those things. Yet we walk this earth feeling like an unconnected, isolated individual.

Here is the source of action and thought. Here is the source of the highest form of inspiration. Emerson wrote, "We lie in the lap of immense intelligence, which makes us organs of its activity and receivers of its truth."

When we recognize justice or truth or goodness, we are not creating it. We are not putting it there, but merely opening to a perception of something that already exists. We allow ourselves (or not) to receive the recognition. We do not make it so by our acknowledgement.

Decisions, opinions, conclusions — these are deliberate acts. But when you look at a flower, whether or not you perceive its color is not up to you. Perception is not under your voluntary control. The deliberate acts of our minds can be disputed, but perception is final and undeniable.

If I perceive something and point it out to someone else, they will perceive it also. And even if I am the first human to ever notice it, I have opened the way for future generations to notice it forevermore.

Although perceptions can be shared, what is perceived is always new, always now. Relying on old philosophies or dogmas misses the fact that all of the universe is being created now, and you need not rely on anybody else to tell you what is. You can receive your knowing directly.

When a person recognizes the truth of something, all former teachings crumble to dust and blow away. The source is eternally now, and dissolves all past and future in its ever-emanating center.

If a person claims to know of divine matters but uses ancient language from another country, do not believe it. Why worship the past? The truth is here, now, as fully and completely as it has ever been. You need no ancient description of the color of the sky; you only need to look up. You can describe it however you want to describe it. Memorizing former descriptions misses the point entirely.

Do not be hesitant. Do not cower in shame or fear. Don't quote some wise man of former ages. Say boldly what *you* perceive now.

Let us hope we do not always think so highly of ancient teachings and obsolete languages. We are like children who memorize rules and ideas, struggling to remember the exact words. Later, when they come to understand more about the world, they can throw away those words and perceive the truths for themselves, saying it just as well from their own present understanding, in their own words. Let us do the same.

"If we live truly," wrote Emerson, "we shall see truly." Live a deeply honest life, and you will perceive what is. Then what old wisdoms need to be remembered? When you live truly, your experience will be original and new. Your experience can and will be a continual surprise and delight.

A deeply honest person does not remind you of anyone else. An authentic person's experience will be utterly unique and singular. Living in honesty, you will not be following any known path because you are *making* a path. You will have no fear. You will have no hope. "Fear and hope are alike beneath it." You will have a tranquility and serenity as you gaze upon the immensity of universal causation.

All time, all space, all distance, all things will be seen through as inconsequential. A rigorous, unrelenting, bold honesty is the path to that ultimate level of perception.

THE WORLD AS IT IS

To clearly see the need for this philosophy of self-reliance, all you need to do is look at our modern world. We are, by and large, timid and easily disheartened. The truth scares us. Death scares us. The future scares us. And we are afraid of each other.

What we want is for someone to rise up and make things right, but what we see is that most people are seriously lacking real personal power. They're passive. They lack a strong sense of purpose. They whine. They feel entitled to much more than their contribution merits. They have no backbone, no guts, no character.

Why? Because they've been beaten down by the opinions of others. They've *conformed*. And in conforming, they've lost their connection to their own selves.

We have all done it. We have tried to avoid the battlefield where truth fights it out with the dark forces. To avoid the battle, we conform. We go along to get along. We fear failure and we fear doing something original. If a young person does well in high school and doesn't go on to a good college, we fear for her future.

If a young businessman fails, we think he is ruined. This is ridiculous. I am ruined or not, beaten or not, depending on what I say to myself. If I boldly think strongly, I'll pick myself up and go on.

With this attitude, I can try and fail at many things and come out all right. If I took the attitude of our society to heart, I would give up at the first sign of failure, climb into a bottle, and complain loudly for the rest of my life.

We are not victims, we are *creators*. Maybe some great teacher will come along who will reveal to us our own power. The teacher would tell us *we must detach ourselves* from our reliance on the values and opinions of our culture. We must become independent. We must become self-reliant. If we would trust ourselves, we would find our powers multiplied. We have come to put the world right, and should be *embarrassed* by the sympathy of others.

The moment you take genuine self-sourced and original action, nobody will pity you. They will admire and emulate you, now and in generations to come.

REVOLUTION

We need a revolution — a *self-reliance revolution* — a new level of trust in the divinity within each of us. Here are some areas where the revolution can be started in your own life:

1. LIVE IN THE PRESENT

Time doesn't exist at the center of all things, as the universe emanates from the core this instant. It is perfect at every moment — just what it is, complete, whole, and right now.

But we habitually ignore the present. We regret the past or yearn for it; we strain our minds to perceive the future; we dismiss the wonder of what is here now.

There is one elemental truth that you must understand now, and re-understand every day: You can't be happy or strong until you live in the present, beyond time.

The ever-present creation is always *dynamic*, always new. This eternal life-source, when it is flowing through you, will be shut down by retiring, by attainment, by ending the quest and deciding you now have "The Answer." It is opened back up again by re-entering the ever-changing river of existence. As Emerson put it, the soul *becomes*.

When you are present and becoming, you are one with the river, and so your actions have power. But hold still, and your power vanishes.

Ride that ever-flowing emanation with your deep honesty, and you are more powerful than kings and countries. People will appear to bend to you, to follow you, but they are not follow-ing *you* — they become the same sun as you are and shine forth with the same light.

Honesty is *reality*. Things are as real as they are honest.

Every honest action reveals a quality, an excellence, and we can't help but respect and admire it.

From this point forward, let us restrain our impulse to wander, to imitate, to envy. Let's look right here and express whatever we feel needs to be expressed the way we feel it ought to be expressed. We will "stun and astonish" the less honest with our simple expression of truth. They don't need to look any further than you: The divine pulse is right here, shining out of you into their face and it makes them feel an incomprehensible shock of recognition.

Next to the richness you are floating in, everything else is shabby and petty. Dive into your ocean within to swim in your indescribable wealth rather than trying to beg a cup of water from someone else.

2. SOLITUDE: A KEY

The ocean within can best be reached through solitude. The pressures, the desires, the opinions, the complaints, of others — even if they love you — only cloud and obscure your vision. Solitude allows the dust to settle and the air to clear. Then you can see truly. Then you can attain the independence and strength and clarity that you will require if you wish to retain your honesty while among people. Otherwise, your human inclination is to acquire the notions and prejudices of your friends and family.

Solitude will free your mind and ears and soul from the constant, unimportant interruptions. Learn to distance yourself from too much entanglement in the problems or goals of others. Certainly shine light where it may help, but their goals and problems are *theirs*, and yours are yours, and keeping that distinction is the only way you can keep your self-reliance.

Remember this: Getting caught in the web of others can only be done with your consent. You have given your consent out of weakness.

But no more.

Your solitude and your deep honesty will strengthen you and guide your attention vitally and healthfully.

3. RIGHT SPEECH

Another key in the quest for deep honesty is to simply try to speak the truth.

Up until now, you have sometimes expressed agreement where you really disagreed, you have occasionally gone along with what you knew was wrong, you have failed to correct mistaken assumptions, and you have restrained your honesty to save others' feelings. You have shut yourself off from your own freedom and power in order to keep someone safe from a painful truth, or merely to keep them liking you. You have taken the golden heart of the universe and traded it for a "benefit" which it is beneath you to desire.

Throw away your pretense and enter reality. Say to the people you know: "I must be myself. I cannot break myself any longer for you." No longer hide your likes and dislikes. Trust that "what is deep is holy." Do and say what truly and deeply delights you. Do and say what makes you feel serene and content and strong and free happy in your heart.

As Emerson put it, "I will do strongly before the sun and moon whatever inly rejoices me and the heart appoints." Not what superficially titillates, but what resonates with bliss at the deepest and highest within you.

Emerson suggests you say to your friends and family, "If you are noble, I will love you; if you are not, I will not hurt you and myself by hypocritical attentions. If you are true, but not in the same truth with me, cleave to your companions; I will seek my own. I do this not selfishly but humbly and truly. It is alike your interest, and mine, and all men's, however long we have dwelt in lies, to live in truth."

This new way of being, this discipline to speak the truth, will sometimes seem excessively harsh. But if you follow the path of honesty, you will ultimately enter the flow of the river — you will ultimately live in reality instead of the tangle of lying, misleading, and pretending that passes for "normal."

Yes, your honesty will cause pain. But will you sell your freedom and power to save someone from an unpleasant feeling? Especially when the feeling is an appropriate response to reality?

In time, if the person will consent to look, they will perceive the truth too, and thus may begin a life of honesty.

The path of authenticity and self-reliance is unusual. People may find it strange and bewildering. To others it may seem as though you have rejected *all* rules simply because you do not conform to the rules of your culture. But the discipline of honesty has its own strict code and profound principles, and if anyone thinks this is an easy path, let him try to keep the regimen for one day, and he will be set straight.

Emerson wrote, "Truly it demands something godlike in him who has cast off the common motives of humanity and has ventured to trust himself for a taskmaster. High be his heart, faithful his will, clear his sight, that he may in good earnest be doctrine, society, law, to himself, that a simple purpose may be to him as strong as iron necessity is to others."

4. PRAYERS

When you pray for anything but the good of all, you are out of touch. Praying for some special favor is a demonstration of the lack of self-trust. That kind of prayer arises out of a lack of knowledge about the unity of all things.

Prayer, if engaged in at all, should be a "contemplation of the facts of life from the highest point of view." It is the monologue of a grateful soul. It is the universe acknowledging itself.

When you live as an open expression of the mystery and grandeur of the universe, you will not beg for private favors in your prayers. You will see all action as prayer. Do not miss this point. Deep honesty will reveal the true way to pray: Take action.

Another form of misguided prayer is regretting the past. If there is some action you can take that will help the situation, then take it. Otherwise, let it go and come back to the present.

And sympathy falls into the same category. We sit down and pat the hands of those who bring trouble on themselves instead of speaking the truth boldly "in rough electric shocks" that might jar them out of their fog and self-created illusions and put them in touch with their own powerful soul.

The secret of success is simply this: Take pleasure in self-derived work. "Welcome evermore to gods and men is the self-helping man." People love and admire him because he does not need their love and admiration. We celebrate his triumphs because he persevered when everyone was against him.

Not only are our prayers an expression of a "disease of the will" but those principles we live by are an expression of an equally pathetic "disease of the intellect."

For the most part, when I speak to someone, I am alone because I am not likely to be speaking to a real person. I'm not likely to meet the universe expressing itself through him. No. He will be following some creed or other, not of his own creation. He will be relying on the external rules created by others rather than trusting himself. He will recite "truths" he has borrowed from others.

But each soul is an entirely new classification. Not a new member of an already-existing class. A new *class*. Each person is original — or at least should be! But people are, for the most part, followers. They do not create or initiate genuine actions, but copy and regurgitate and recycle.

When an un-self-reliant person finds some new philosophy, she will think it is the end-all, be-all, the all-encompassing truth. It is natural to feel an enthusiasm for new ideas, new systems — at least for awhile, because you can feel the new philosophy has expanded your understanding and the reach of your mind. A self-reliant soul, however, will outgrow the system and go beyond it. The weak mind will stop seeking and consider the new philosophy the only truth and will refuse to understand how anyone else could see the light without the particular teachings of this one master.

But the light will shine on any open mind. It makes no narrow discriminations. It only requires honesty to open the door, and it will happily beam bright and warm into the humblest shack.

If our follower would become honest and self-reliant, the master's philosophy would crack at the edges and fall away, allowing the light to shine directly into the heart of this newly-opened soul.

5. TRAVELING

Another area in which to start this revolution of self-reliance is with the habit of traveling. It is ironic that we will travel thousands of miles to see great architecture rather than staying home and building our own great works — something the architects of these great foreign buildings obviously did.

Of course there is a place for travel, but not as a way of finding anything. You take yourself with you wherever you go, and if you are not at ease in your own home, you will not be at ease anywhere else.

If you hope to find something greater than your own surroundings when you go traveling, you will be sadly disappointed. Greatness is everywhere, even where you are, if you would open your eyes and look. As Emerson wrote, "Traveling is a fool's paradise."

You may travel to get away from yourself, but no matter how far you go, when you wake up in this new place and look in the mirror, there you are. You can't escape yourself.

6. IMITATION

The sixth area ripe for a self-reliant revolution is the disease of imitation, which is a kind of traveling of the intellect. We admire styles and ideas that seem foreign, from another country or another time. But in each place and time, great works were created then and there. The model was in the mind of the artist and not anywhere or anywhen else.

Remember this: Beauty and magnificence are as near to you as to anyone, and if you would decorate your house and your mind with what fits your own disposition, your own tastes, your own place and time, you will find it extraordinary and wonderful, fitting and satisfying.

"Insist on yourself," wrote Emerson, "never imitate." You can express your own talents every moment, and those talents have been accumulating power and refinement your entire life. But when you try to imitate or adopt the talents of another, you have only a superficial "half-possession."

Whatever you can do *best*, nobody can teach you but your own inner light and your own work and practice. Where was the genius who could have taught Shakespeare? Who could have taught Thoreau or Einstein or Edison? Every great soul is unique and original. What makes Thoreau great is that very part he could not borrow from anyone else. A new Thoreau could never be made by the study of Thoreau.

Do the task that calls to you and you cannot be too optimistic about the outcome. There is, right in this moment, a great work inside you — a work as awe-inspiring as the Great Pyramid, the 5th symphony, or the Theory of Relativity, but different from them all. The source of the universe is capable of infinite expression, and if it has the use of a new mouthpiece (from your newly-acquired deep honesty), it will not repeat itself. Why would it? If you had an infinite number of different things to say, why would you ever repeat yourself? Any true expression that flows through you will be wholly new and original.

And if you think you are not that great, that you aren't capable of originality or outstandingness, think about this: If you have the power to understand what another great soul has expressed — if you understand those great words, if you grasp the beauty of a painting, if you recognize the genius of a piece of music — surely you also have the power to answer in the same tone of voice as an equal. If you are up to that level of understanding, you are on an equal plane, and can reply in kind.

You may not know how to paint or write music, but you have a genius of expression with which you *can* reply. You and I have greatness inside us waiting to get out. Throw open the gates with the transcendent power of honesty.

7. WHAT REALLY IMPROVES

The self-reliance revolution needs to revamp our ideas about improvement. You cannot improve "society." It changes, but the change is not improvement — for everything that becomes better, something becomes worse. We get new forms of entertainment and they waste hours of our time, distancing us from our loved ones, making us feel isolated and alone in a world full of people. We get electricity and the light bulb, and it throws our carefully-evolved biological system, attuned for eons to the earth's cycles of light and dark, out of balance. We get new modes of transportation and lose some health from our drop in exercise. We get labor-saving devices and then *both* parents have to work to pay for it all.

HOW TO BE HAPPY

Circumstances are insignificant and relatively inconsequential. We look to things, to property, to external situations to make us happy, to make us good, to make us feel satisfied or redeemed. These things cannot be gotten from circumstances or ownership of anything.

We have a tendency to make the mistake of measuring each other by what we *have* rather than by what we have *become*. But property is superficial. When you act from your center, you will probably acquire property, but it doesn't matter because the important gain is not material goods but a stronger character. You have become a more excellent channel — a finer instrument — for the universal will.

Another form of our misguided reliance on external property is our thirst for the agreement of others. We want *large* groups of people to believe as we do, and we feel stronger every time a new convert joins our group, whatever our group may be: vegetarian, democrat, positive thinker, whatever.

But the nature of wisdom and power works in exactly the opposite way. You gain access to the universal expression only by *letting go* of the opinions, customs, rules, and systems of others and standing alone, original, self-reliant, self-trusting, and self-sourced.

If you would release your fearful clinging to the wisdom of others and throw yourself on your own wits, you would instantly right yourself like a ship heeled over and suddenly becoming upright again.

Your balance returns. Your power resurges. Your weakness was only caused by your lack of confidence in your own wisdom.

Don't rely on luck, either. Trust in the law of cause and effect. Do your work. Speak the truth. Live your life with deep honesty, and you have made luck irrelevant. The causes will produce their effects, luck or no luck.

And if some lucky good fortune comes your way — you win the lottery, your annoying neighbor moves away, the value of your stock suddenly rises — you may be tempted to think luck is on your side. Don't believe it. External circumstances have no lasting value. Your deep honesty and *only* your deep honesty can bring you true satisfaction and contentment.

ABOUT THE TRANSLATOR

Adam Khan is the author of the books, *Self-Help Stuff That Works*, *Principles For Personal Growth* (now being used as a textbook for a college course in San Diego), *What Difference Does It Make: How the Sexes Differ and What You Can Do About It*, *Viewfinder: How to Change the Way You Look at Things*, *Cultivating Fire: How to Keep Your Motivation White Hot*, and *Antivirus For Your Mind*. He's also creator and webmaster of the web site, youmeworks.com and he blogs at crushpessimism.com and moodraiser.com.

Adam has been published in *Prevention Magazine*, *Cosmopolitan*, *Body Bulletin*, *Your Personal Best Newsletter*, *Wisdom*, *Think and Grow Rich Newsletter*, the *Success Strategies* newsletter, and he was a regular columnist for *At Your Best* (a Rodale Press publication) for seven years where his monthly column was voted the readers' favorite. He would love to hear from you. Write him at adam@youmeworks.com.

SOMEWHAT BETTER THAN WHIM

"I would write on the lintels of the door-post, *Whim*. I hope it is somewhat better than whim at last, but we cannot spend the day in explanation."

– Ralph Waldo Emerson, *Self-Reliance*

I'VE THOUGHT A LOT about this essay and what it means, and what follows are a few of my observations and thoughts on it.

First of all, have you ever wondered why artists and geniuses often seem so eccentric? Eccentric means "deviating from recognized standards." In other words, "not like anybody else."

I think it's possible that in order to be original and creative you would have to resist the normal temptation to conform.

And this would not just apply to conforming to *other* peoples' standards and *society's* standards, but even your *own* standards. This rebellion against *standards* might make you more capable of being creative. It would help make you capable of thinking of things nobody else has thought of, or thinking in *ways* nobody else has thought before.

In other words, maybe that's how you would get to that state where you can create original work: By following your whim.

So even though you've already decided to go *this* way, at the moment you feel like going *that* way, so you go that way. You're following your whim. And like Emerson said, hopefully it's somewhat better than whim, but we can't spend the day in explanation.

That's how you could get outside the standards, the conforming, the already-having-been-created. Because really, that's all you're doing when you're conforming: You're *imitating* something that has already been created, whether it's your own previous plans or your own previous decisions about how things should be done, or your own *previous* beliefs or the beliefs of our society or of your parents, or whatever — *conforming* means following a pattern previously created.

To follow your own path, to be self-reliant, to have integrity, what do you follow if you don't follow convention and you don't mechanically follow your own rules or previous plans? You would follow your whim. That would be the other thing you could follow. I don't know what else it could be. Call it intuition or your inner voice.

And I think Emerson is right. It *would* make you original and creative. "Creative," meaning "coming up with stuff nobody has ever done before or thought before." And "original," meaning essentially the same thing.

And I think there is a difference between "following your whim" and "not doing what other people do." I do not think these are the same.

You often see people who are very rebelious. They're contrarians. They do what others don't do. But they're doing *what others don't do* rather than doing something original. They're still responding to something *already* established. That's different than following your whim. That's not the same as following the inner light. And maybe that's why contrarians don't usually seem creative or happy; they just seem annoying and rebellious.

It's also possible that you can't come up with something original and creative by trying to come up with something original and creative. It's possible you would only be able to do it following your whim. Just following what you really want to do at the moment.

Trusting Yourself

In one section of *Self-Reliance*, Emerson says your own lack of trust in yourself causes you to want to imitate others, or in some other way not be yourself.

Then in another part of the essay he says society tries to make you conform, to be what you're not, and it uses scorn and disapproval to control you and keep you from being yourself.

I just watched a movie last night, a mini-series called *Elvis* (starring Jonathan Rhys Meyers) and there on the screen were Emerson's principles demonstrated with such stark poignancy it felt like Emerson had directed the movie.

In one of the early scenes, when Elvis was making his first recording, the producer (Sam Phillips, who was a one-man show — owner, recording engineer, producer, manager) came into the recording room after Elvis had sung a few songs and said, basically, "What the hell is this? You sound like (and he names some singers), and they already *have* records. People have already heard *them*. I want you to sound like *you*."

In other words, Elvis did exactly what Emerson said people tend to do: He didn't trust himself and was trying to imitate others. He was imitating his favorite singers.

Later, they were taking a break and Elvis was goofing around, just passing the time playing his guitar and singing (in other words, Elvis was accidentally just being himself).

Sam heard it and said, "That's great!" and recorded it. And that was Elvis' first hit. It was *alive*, it was unique, and it was completely Elvis.

Later in his career, after he had hired a new manager and before going on tour, Elvis went to Sun Records to say goodbye to Sam.

After Sam wished him well, he told Elvis, "They're going to try to clean you up, to slick you up. You just be who you are, and you'll be all right."

In other words, "the world will try to make you conform to what *they* want you to be." Elvis, unfortunately, did not follow this advice.

Sam was right. The Money Machine tried to turn him into something he wasn't. Elvis was pushed by his manager to do stupid movies — movies that Elvis didn't want to do — and pushed him into singing songs he didn't really like, and singing them in a way that just wasn't him.

And guess what? If you do enough of what you don't want to do, if you aren't motivated, if it doesn't excite you, and if you have to continually be something you're not, you will inevitably feel miserable, no matter how much money and adoring fans you have.

In order to deal with the boredom and unhappiness caused by the perpetual violation of his own integrity, Elvis took uppers to keep him energized and downers to help him sleep, and his life slowly spiraled down into hell.

Then the producer of a television special set up a situation where Elvis could just be himself and do his thing, and he came alive! His performance was outstanding.

I saw that performance and it was the first time I ever had the thought, "Elvis is good." He was great! So charismatic, such a soulful singer and so entertaining.

Prior to that time I never understood how he had become so famous, because by the time I was listening to music, Elvis had already sold his soul. He had conformed to what others thought he should be.

But this single performance revived him for only a short time. Then he went back to conforming. His manager and his father convinced him he needed to conform to their wishes. He needed to go back to doing what they thought was best. And he went back to being miserable.

Let this be a lesson for all of us. The world *whips us with its displeasure*, as Emerson wrote, if we don't conform. It has always done so, and it will always do so. It will never stop. It will never let up. It tries to make us conform to standards we didn't choose or create.

And our own lack of courage does the same thing from within, hollowing out our own self-trust and leaving but the shales and husks of our real selves.

But it doesn't have to be this way. We can be our honest selves, we can follow our own way, and we can be happy. It will take courage and commitment, but it can be done. Gandhi did it. Lincoln did it. Emerson did it. My wife does it. And you and I can do it too.

Being Alive

One the most influential books I've ever read on integrity and self-reliance is Lewis Andrews' *To Thine Own Self Be True*.

Andrews is a psychologist and his main message is that many of our most common "psychological problems" have their roots in unethical behavior.

In other words, one valid and productive approach to problems like anxiety, depression, guilt, and anger problems is to ask, "Where am I violating my own integrity?" And Andrews presents a good deal of evidence from scientific studies to validate this approach.

I have found the idea personally helpful. It has been productive to respond to emotional issues by first checking my own integrity.

For example, if I feel bored and restless, it's likely I am doing something I don't really feel is important but feel I *should* do (or something someone has convinced me is a good idea), but my heart isn't in it.

Elvis was doing that with his music and movies. And what was the result? He suffered from a deep boredom and the empty feeling of just going through the motions. He didn't feel engaged in his own life.

It was an *integrity* issue. He was not being himself. He was doing what he was told. He was conforming. He *thought* he was doing the right thing, making sure he had the money to take care of his mother. It would have taken courage to rely on himself and not just do what the authorities told him he should do. But what if it didn't work? What if it failed?

Following his own way would have been risky, for sure. But he would have been happier. And he probably would have created more original, creative work.

Self-Reliance is Not for Sissies

If you were going to make a list of outstanding examples of truly self-reliant people who followed their own way, who would you put on the list? At the top of my list would be Gandhi, Lincoln, and Socrates. Many people would add Martin Luther King, Jr. and Jesus.

Besides being moral exemplars, what else do they have in common? They were all assassinated, executed, or forced to kill themselves.

The point of this grim history lesson is that *self-reliance is not for sissies*. If you follow your whim, if you stay true to yourself, if you trust yourself as a taskmaster and speak the truth, some people will *really* not like it. Self-reliance is not a way to become popular.

On the other hand, other people will be strongly attracted to your self-reliance and originality, so it's not a road to complete unpopularity either. All five of the exemplars above had lots of popular support. But they didn't win over *everyone* and didn't even try. They had enemies, and that is inevitable when you follow your own path. Some people won't like it.

When you feel a conflict between living with self-reliance and living a frictionless life, or when you are motivated by your own "somewhat better than whim" and people think it's wrong or offensive, you should remind yourself of this: *You're not alone* and you're in very good company, historically speaking.

What Self-Reliance Means

Like many of us, I have a natural tendency to orient myself toward what I'm guessing other people think about what I'm doing. I want people to think well of me. So I'm tempted to participate in "impression management." That is, I am tempted to try to control the impression I'm making on others. I want people to know I'm a good person, so I want to do things that would make them think that about me.

When I worked as a waiter in the banquet department of a nice restaurant, I regularly worked with a small group of other waiters.

Since we were all on the same tip pool, we were acutely aware of each other's work ethic. If I was working hard and the person next to me was slacking, it would bother me because we were splitting our tip money equally. And I knew others felt the same.

I remember one night working in a room *by myself* after the guests had left. I was clearing and resetting the room while my teammates were doing the same in another room, and I wanted to make sure if one of them came in they would see I had been working hard, so without really thinking about it, I found myself doing those things that would be the most obvious demonstrations of productive work, as opposed to working efficiently.

Then I noticed what I was doing.

I was studying *Self-Reliance* in earnest at the time, trying to notice when I was self-reliant and when I wasn't.

One of my favorite lines from the essay is: "What I must do is all that concerns me, not what the people think."

As soon as I noticed what I was doing, I returned myself to my own integrity — I started doing what *I* thought ought to be done, doing what *I* thought was best — and I immediately *felt* different. When I got home that night, I wrote about it. I said I felt "more solid, more grounded, more centered. My orientation shifted from *impression management* to doing what I thought needed to be done in order to do a good job."

That was the first time I understood what the term "self-reliance" really meant. All the time I had been studying the book, I'd actually wondered why Emerson titled it *Self-Reliance* when it is really an essay about personal integrity.

But that night I *got* it, and I realized that's a really good word for what Emerson was describing.

When I shifted my orientation from "what my fellow workers might think" to "what I thought was best, what was true for me, what I would be satisfied with," I was relying on my *own* judgment about my actions as opposed to trying to rely on what I was *guessing* other people might think.

Oriented to other people like that is a very insecure foundation and I think that's why I felt so much more "solid and grounded and center-ed" when I shifted to what *I* thought was best.

It's more secure because I *know* what *I* think is best. It may not actually *be* best in some absolute way, but I am certain that *I* think it's best.

And I'm not sure what others think is best (or if what they think is best is *really* best) and I know it's not really possible to ever know for sure what they really think. So it's an intrinsic-ally insecure foundation.

"Self-reliance" is a *great* word for being true to yourself.

Another insight I had at the same time is that "guessing what others think" is the thing that competes most directly with my integrity. I'm not tempted to steal; I'm not tempted to cheat. Those impulses don't really compete in me with integrity. But my concern about what others think, my desire to control what others think and to make them think I'm a good person — *that* is something I used to do a lot, and still feel tempted to do even today.

The mental activity of guessing what others think competes directly with the mental activity of being self-reliant. It is the *strongest* competition with being true to myself, which is one of the main points Emerson makes in the essay. The world whips you with its displeasure *when you don't conform.*

And concern about what *others* think is not the only thing that competes with self-reliance. We also need to be aware of our natural tendency to want to conform to what we have previously said or done. Not just because *others* expect it, but because we expect it of ourselves. We have an inner drive to be consistent, to conform to our own personal history.

The author, Robert Cialdini, wrote an outstanding book, *Influence,* which is about what makes people comply, what makes people say "yes." He wasn't writing about self-reliance, but when he described the six principles of influence, one of them was "commitment and consistency."

What he wrote is based on sociological and psychological studies. And coming from this completely different orientation, what he and other researchers have discovered unambiguously confirms what Emerson wrote.

In Cialdini's description of the *commitment and consistency* principle, he said: "It is, quite simply, our nearly obsessive desire to be (and to appear) consistent with what we have already done. Once we have made a choice or taken a stand, we will encounter personal and interpersonal pressures to behave consistently with that commitment. Those pressures will cause us to respond in ways that justify our earlier decision."

The pressure comes from within and from without. Internally, you feel the need to be consistent. Externally, you feel pressure because the world might "misunderstand" you.

In one of the most quoted passages from *Self-Reliance*, Emerson wrote: "A foolish consistency is the hobgoblin of little minds, adored by little statesmen and philosophers and divines. With consistency a great soul has simply nothing to do. He may as well concern himself with his shadow on the wall. Out upon your guarded lips! Sew them up with pack-thread, do. Else if you would be a man speak what you think today in words as hard as cannonballs, and tomorrow speak what tomorrow thinks in hard words again, though it contradict everything you said today. Ah, then, exclaim the aged ladies, you shall be sure to be misunderstood! Misunderstood! It is a right fool's word. Is it so bad then to be misunderstood? Pythagoras was misunderstood, and Socrates and Jesus, and Luther, and Copernicus, and Galileo, and Newton, and every pure and wise spirit that ever took flesh. To be great is to be misunderstood."

Michael Karnjanaprakorn, the CEO and co-founder of *Skillshare* (a community marketplace that facilitates offline learning experiences in communities around the world, allowing people to host and take classes with each other), wrote: "Mark Zuckerberg was misunderstood when he introduced the newsfeed and turned down a billion dollars. Steve Jobs was misunderstood, and Cory Booker, and Richard Branson, and David Simon, and Kayne West. If you're not being misunderstood, then you're not shattering the status quo."

And when he says "misunderstood" he means *criticized* and misunderstood.

We don't want to be criticized, and we want the approval and admiration of others. What are the simplest, most instinctive, commonplace solutions? To conform and to imitate.

But Mark Frauenfelder agrees with Emerson's opening salvo — that if you want to be great, if you want to be original, if you want to be at peace with yourself, you cannot imitate.

Why do we even *want* to imitate? Because we already know X is popular. People like it. It is successful. We want people to like us too, and we want to be successful, so the most natural solution is to imitate what is already successful.

When you do something that has never been done before, *you don't know* if people will like it. How can you proceed into the unknown like that?

Emerson gives us the answer: "To believe your own thought, to believe that what is true for you in your private heart is true for all men — that is genius."

Frauenfelder wrote: "It's a waste of time to imitate, to do something other people can do as good or better than you. I make the media that I want to consume. I started bOING bOING as a print zine because it was the kind of zine I wanted to read. Boing Boing was the blog I always wanted. MAKE was the do-it-yourself magazine I wanted to subscribe to. It's fine to be inspired by others, but if you imitate others, you will never find out who you are."

Emerson points out that most of us dismiss our own original thought *only because the thought is ours.* We respect the original thoughts of "great thinkers" without realizing that what made that thinker great is that she *didn't* dismiss her own original thoughts.

I'll leave you with a couple final gems from *Self-Reliance* that I believe sum up his message in two sentences: "A man should learn to detect and watch that gleam of light which flashes across his mind from within, more than the luster of the firmament of bards and sages..."

"Trust thyself: every heart vibrates to that iron string."

Made in the USA
San Bernardino, CA
31 May 2015